Piano • Vocal • Guitar

Acoustic C
44 Songs Of The '60s And '70s

ISBN 0-7935-4587-0

HAL•LEONARD®
CORPORATION

7777 W. BLUEMOUND RD. P.O. BOX 13819 MILWAUKEE, WI 53213

Visit Hal Leonard Online at
www.halleonard.com

CONTENTS

AMERICAN PIE

Words and Music by
DON McLEAN

9

day the mu-sic died. And they were sing-in'.

CODA

This-'ll be the day _ that I___ die. ___

Additional Lyrics

2. Now for ten years we've been on our own,
And moss grows fat on a rollin' stone
But that's not how it used to be
When the jester sang for the king and queen
In a coat he borrowed from James Dean
And a voice that came from you and me
Oh and while the king was looking down,
The jester stole his thorny crown
The courtroom was adjourned,
No verdict was returned
And while Lenin read a book on Marx
The quartet practiced in the park
And we sang dirges in the dark
The day the music died
We were singin'... bye-bye... etc.

3. Helter-skelter in the summer swelter
The birds flew off with a fallout shelter
Eight miles high and fallin' fast,
it landed foul on the grass
The players tried for a forward pass,
With the jester on the sidelines in a cast
Now the half-time air was sweet perfume
While the sergeants played a marching tune
We all got up to dance
But we never got the chance
'Cause the players tried to take the field,
The marching band refused to yield
Do you recall what was revealed
The day the music died
We started singin'... bye-bye... etc.

4. And there we were all in one place,
A generation lost in space
With no time left to start again
So come on, Jack be nimble, Jack be quick,
Jack Flash sat on a candlestick
'Cause fire is the devil's only friend
And as I watched him on the stage
My hands were clenched in fists of rage
No angel born in hell
Could break that Satan's spell
And as the flames climbed high into the night
To light the sacrificial rite
I saw Satan laughing with delight
The day the music died
He was singin'... bye-bye... etc.

AND I LOVE YOU SO

Words and Music by
DON McLEAN

Moderately slow

1.,3. And I love you
2. And you love me

so,
too,

The peo - ple ask me how,
Your thoughts are just for me,

How I've lived till now,
You set my spir - it free,

I tell them I don't know.
I'm hap - py that you do.

I guess they un - der- stand,
The book of life is brief,

How lone - ly life has been,
And once a page is read,

MCA music publishing

CAROLINA IN MY MIND

Words and Music by
JAMES TAYLOR

In my mind I'm gone to Car - o - li - na.

Can't you see the sun - shine? And

can't you just feel the moon - shine?_____ And ain't it just like a

ANGIE

Words and Music by MICK JAGGER
and KEITH RICHARDS

ANNIE'S SONG

Words and Music by
JOHN DENVER

AT SEVENTEEN

Words and Music by
JANIS IAN

BLACKBIRD

Words and Music by JOHN LENNON
and PAUL McCARTNEY

Black - bird sing-ing in the dead of night___
Black - bird sing-ing in the dead of night ___

Take these bro-ken wings___ and learn to fly;___
Take these sunk-en eyes___ and learn to see;___

All your life_____ you were on - ly wait-ing for this mo-ment to a -
All your life_____ you were on - ly wait-ing for this mo-ment to be

42

CASTLES IN THE AIR

Words and Music by
DON McLEAN

48

COME MONDAY

Words and Music by
JIMMY BUFFETT

COUNTRY ROAD

Words and Music by
JAMES TAYLOR

53

54

55

DON'T LET ME BE LONELY TONIGHT

Words and Music by
JAMES TAYLOR

DUST IN THE WIND

Moderate Folk style

Words and Music by
KERRY LIVGREN

FIRE AND RAIN

Words and Music by
JAMES TAYLOR

FREE BIRD

Words and Music by ALLEN COLLINS
and RONNIE VAN ZANT

MCA music publishing

Lord knows I can't change.

(Instrumental)

Lord, help me, I can't change.

I WILL

Words and Music by JOHN LENNON
and PAUL McCARTNEY

I'LL FOLLOW THE SUN

Words and Music by JOHN LENNON
and PAUL McCARTNEY

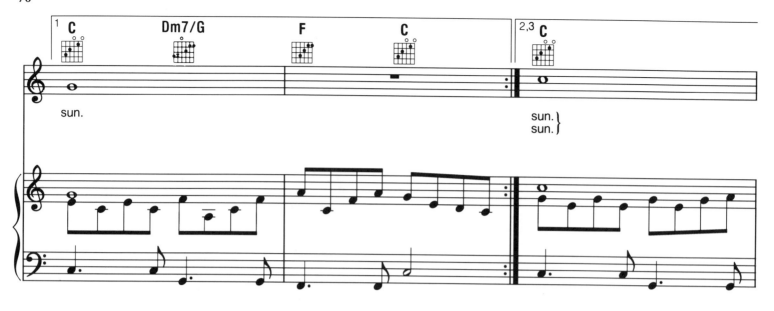

And now the time has come,— And so, my love,— I must go.—

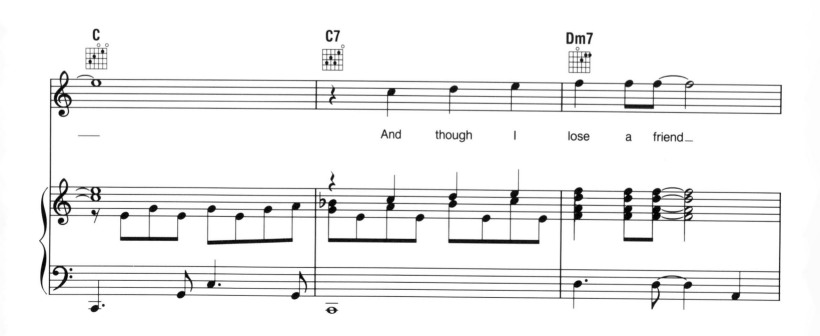

— And though I lose a friend—

I'M LOOKING THROUGH YOU

Words and Music by JOHN LENNON
and PAUL McCARTNEY

I'm look-ing through___ you,
Your lips are mov-

— you,   where did you go?___
-ing,   I can - not___ hear.

Why, tell me why___ did you___ not treat me right?___

Love has a nas - ty hab - it of

dis - ap - pear - ing o - ver night.___ You're think - ing

I'm look - ing through___

IF

Words and Music by
DAVID GATES

Moderately, with feeling

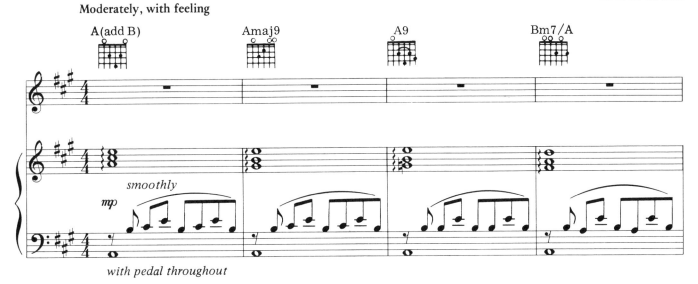

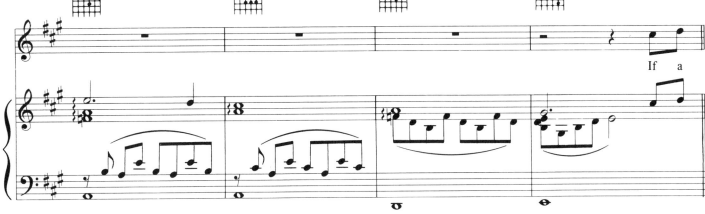

pic - ture paints a thou - sand words,___ then why___ can't I___ paint

man could be two plac - es at___ one time,___ I'd be___ with

I'VE JUST SEEN A FACE

Words and Music by JOHN LENNON
and PAUL McCARTNEY

IF I HAD A HAMMER
(THE HAMMER SONG)

Words and Music by LEE HAYS
and PETE SEEGER

92

LEAVING ON A JET PLANE

Words and Music by
JOHN DENVER

LONG LONG TIME

Words and Music by
GARY B. WHITE

LONGER

Words and Music by
DAN FOGELBERG

Long - er than__ there've been fish - es in the o - cean,
Strong - er than__ an - y moun - tain cath - e - dral.
Through the years__ as the fi - re starts to mel - low,

MAGGIE MAY

Words and Music by ROD STEWART
and MARTIN QUITTENTON

2. You lured me away from home, just to save you from being alone.
You stole my soul, that's a pain I can do without.
All I needed was a friend to lend a guiding hand.
But you turned into a lover, and, Mother, what a lover! You wore me out.
All you did was wreck my bed, and in the morning kick me in the head.
Oh, Maggie, I couldn't have tried any more.

3. You lured me away from home, 'cause you didn't want to be alone.
You stole my heart, I couldn't leave you if I tried.
I suppose I could collect my books and get back to school.
Or steal my Daddy's cue and make a living out of playing pool,
Or find myself a rock and roll band that needs a helpin' hand.
Oh, Maggie, I wish I'd never seen your face. **(To Coda)**

ME AND BOBBY McGEE

Words and Music by KRIS KRISTOFFERSON
and FRED FOSTER

110

MY SWEET LADY

Words and Music by
JOHN DENVER

NEW KID IN TOWN

Words and Music by JOHN DAVID SOUTHER,
DON HENLEY and GLENN FREY

PLEASE COME TO BOSTON

Words and Music by
DAVE LOGGINS

Now this drift-er's world goes 'round and 'round and I doubt if it's ev-er gon-na stop. But of

all the dreams I've lost or found, and all that I ain't got, I still need to

lean to some bod - y I can sing to.

D. S. al Fine 𝄋

ADDITIONAL LYRICS

Verse 3.
   Please come to L.A. to live forever
   A California life alone is just too hard to build
   I live in a house that looks out over the ocean
   And there's some stars that fell from the sky
   Living up on the hill
   Please come to L.A., she just said no,
   Boy, won't you come home to me.
Repeat Chorus

THE NIGHT THEY DROVE OLD DIXIE DOWN

Words and Music by
ROBBIE ROBERTSON

126

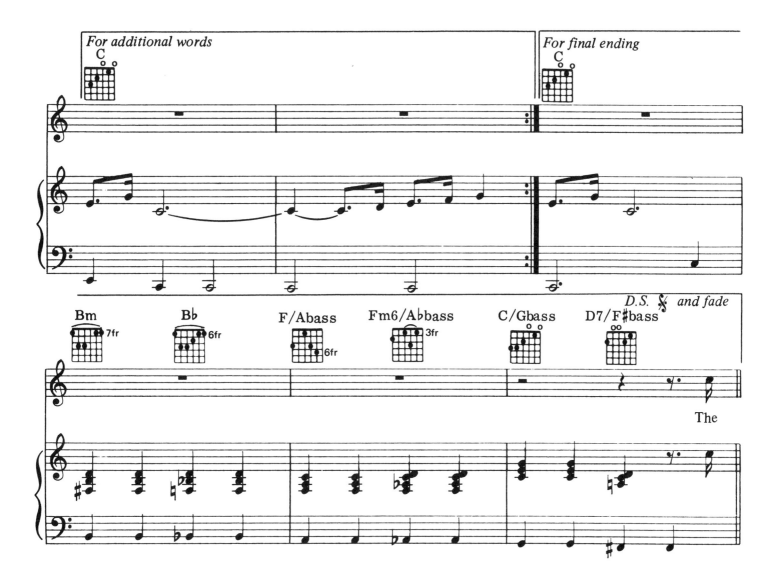

ADDITIONAL WORDS

Back with my wife in Tennessee
When one day she called to me
"Virgil, quick, come see:
There goes Robert E. Lee!"
Now, I don't mind choppin' wood
And I don't care if the money's no good,
Ya take what ya need and ya leave the rest
But they should never have taken
The very best.
(Repeat Chorus)

Like my father before me
I will work the land.
And like my brother above me
Who took a rebel stand.
He was just eighteen, proud and brave,
But a Yankee laid him in his grave,
I swear by the mud below my feet,
You can't raise a Caine back up
When he's in defeat.
(Repeat Chorus with final ending)

NORWEGIAN WOOD
(THIS BIRD HAS FLOWN)

Words and Music by JOHN LENNON
and PAUL McCARTNEY

PART OF THE PLAN

Words and Music by
DAN FOGELBERG

through to you,   some kind of mes-sage comes ___ through, ___   and it says to you:
through to you,   some kind of mes-sage shoots ___ through, ___   and it says to you:

"Love when you can, ___   cry when you have_ to; be who you must, that's a part ___ of the plan._   A-

wait your ar - riv - al ___ with sim - ple sur - viv - al and one day we'll all un - der - stand,

one day we'll all un - der - stand,   one day we'll all un - der - stand."_____

133

ROCKY MOUNTAIN HIGH

Words and Music by JOHN DENVER
and MIKE TAYLOR

ROCKY RACCOON

Words and Music by JOHN LENNON
and PAUL McCARTNEY

144

146

help with good Rock - y's re - vi - val.

STEAMROLLER
(a/k/a STEAMROLLER BLUES)

Words and Music by
JAMES TAYLOR

SUMMER BREEZE

Words and Music by JAMES SEALS
and DASH CROFTS

See the cur - tains hang - in' in the win - dow___ in the eve - ning on a Fri - day night.___
See the pa - per lay - in' on the side - walk, _ a lit - tle mu - sic from the house next door.

A lit - tle light a shin - in' through the win - dow____
So I walk on up to the door - step, ____

____ lets me know ev - 'ry - thing's al - right. ____
____ through the screen and a - cross the floor. ____

Sum-mer breeze_ makes me feel fine,_ blow- in' through the jas - mine in my

SUNSHINE ON MY SHOULDERS

Words by JOHN DENVER
Music by JOHN DENVER, MIKE TAYLOR and DICK KNISS

UNTIL IT'S TIME FOR YOU TO GO

Words and Music by
BUFFY SAINTE-MARIE

Slow Waltz

163

SWEET BABY JAMES

Words and Music by
JAMES TAYLOR

TURN! TURN! TURN!
(TO EVERYTHING THERE IS A SEASON)

Words from the Book of Ecclesiastes
Adaptation and Music by PETE SEEGER

TWO OF US

Words and Music by JOHN LENNON
and PAUL McCARTNEY

1. Two of us, rid - ing no - where, spend - ing some -
2. Two of us, send - ing post - cards, writ - ing let -
3,4. Two of us, wear - ing rain - coats, stand - ing so -

- one's hard - earned pay.
- ers, on my wall.
- lo, in the sun.

VINCENT
(STARRY STARRY NIGHT)

Words and Music by
DON McLEAN

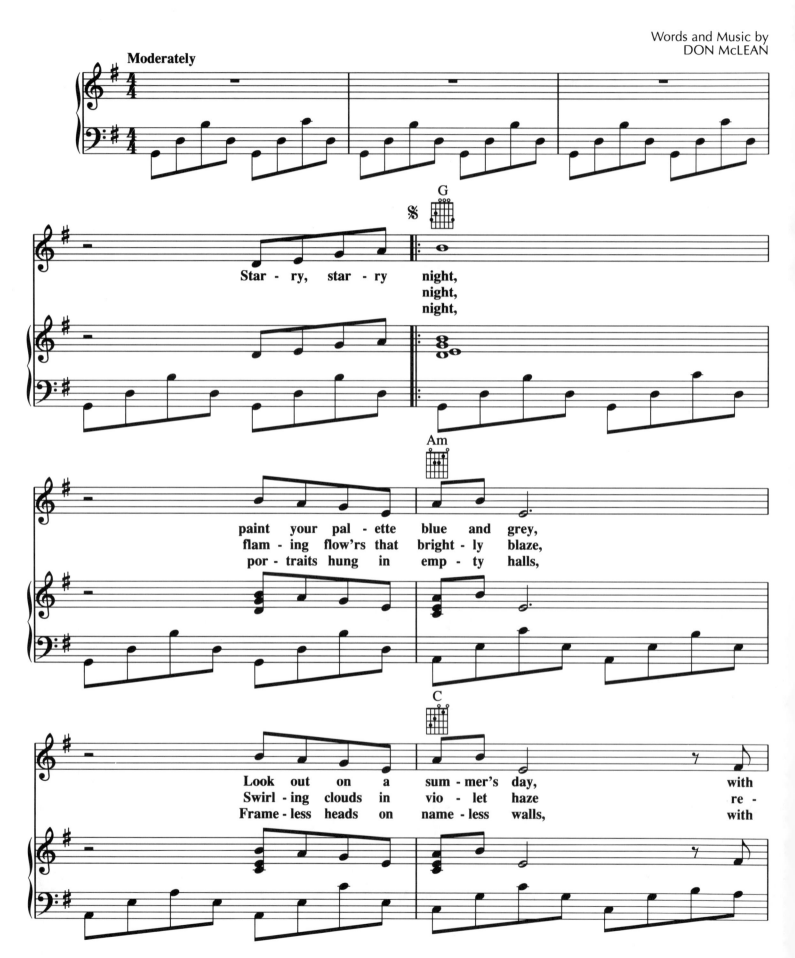

MCA music publishing

178

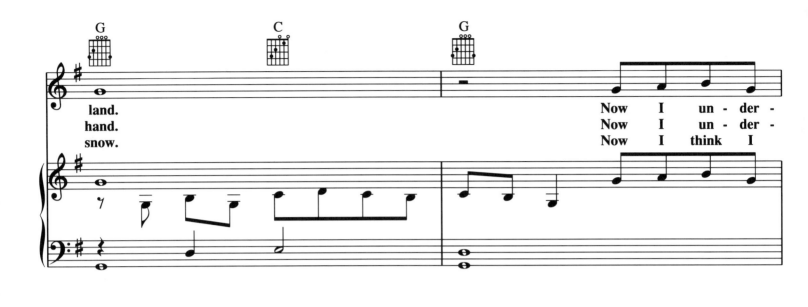

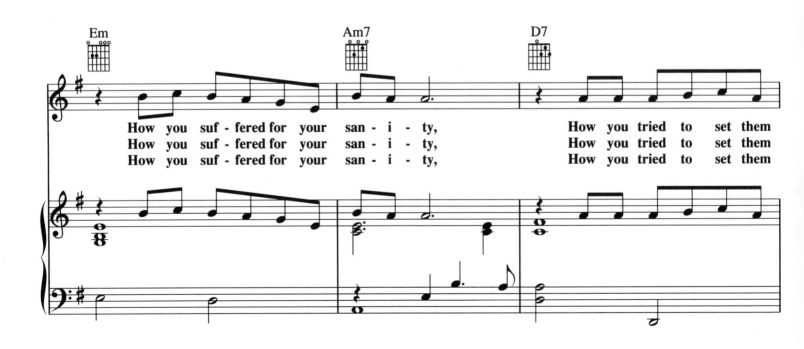

Yesterday

Words and Music by JOHN LENNON
and PAUL McCARTNEY

WE JUST DISAGREE

Words and Music by
JIM KRUEGER

YOU'VE GOT A FRIEND

Words and Music by
CAROLE KING

192